I0337440

DAMAGED
GOD
TONIKA YVONNE WHEELER

Damaged Goods

By Tonika Yvonne Wheeler

Cover illustrated by Cedric Edwards

Designed by Jazzy Kitty Publications

Logo Designs by Andre M. Saunders/Leroy Grayson

Photographs/Illustrations: Cedric Edwards, www. aahgsutah.org, Tammy Saiz at Starlitevisions starlitegodess01@yahoo.com

Editor: Anelda L. Attaway

ISBN 978-0-9892656-0-7

Published by Jazzy Kitty Publishing dba Jazzy Kitty Publications. Utilizing Microsoft and Adobe Publishing Software. Utilizing Adobe and Microsoft Publishing Software.

ACKNOWLEDGMENTS

To my parents and siblings: Thanks for your unconditional love and support. Mom, thank you for encouraging me to write.

To my daughter: I love you unconditionally. You are wise beyond your years. Thanks for your love and for always encouraging me to follow my dreams.

To my husband: Thanks for your support. And for not being afraid to go on my crazy dream ride with me.

To my extended family and friends: Thanks for your years of support and love.

To DeLaw you were always my #1 fan, R.I.P my dear friend and my family who've received their wings; I miss each one of you. Until we meet again.

DEDICATION

For:

Those that life's been everything but kind to.

TABLE OF CONTENTS

TABLE OF CONTENTS

TABLE OF CONTENTS

INTRODUCTION

Damaged Goods celebrates the whirlwinds of life through a collection of poetry written by Tonika Yvonne Wheeler. "Damaged Goods" is her debut 'Poetry' book. The author illustrates the dark sides of life with momentary illumination. Bitterness and spitefulness doesn't have a color, gender, age, or social status. Nor is immunity gained from life's whirlwinds based off one's moral stance or bleeding heart.

"I'll never get married again!" uttered a once thoughtful male friend going through a taxing divorce.

The author sat listening to his non-stop verbal jabs at his soon to be ex-wife, women, and marriage.

"You're Damaged Goods," the author replied.

But the good thing about damaged goods is they can always be refurbished. And sometimes the refurbished goods work better than the one that's never been damaged. Or does it?

LIFE'S ADVERSITIES

Life's adversities

Stormy dark clouds

Appear rapidly

Unexpected roadblocks

Natural human catastrophes

Struggles with realities

Giving all of your energy

For another's mental and physical growth

Leeches taking…taking…taking

You giving, giving, giving

Giving so much of yourself

You have nothing left

Life's adversities

Appearing so rapidly

Natural human catastrophes

Within these pages

Life's stories

Passions

Adversities

Fallacies

Life's…Realities

DAMAGED GOODS

DAMAGED GOODS

She was excited about high school graduation
And oh yea, she's in like with some boy too
Deliberately pushes her buttons, constantly in a fight

She told her bff, "He'd never do anything to hurt me."
Relationship severed;
she foolishly thought they'd remain friends
Until the day, he forced her onto Satan's sheets

She closed her eyes trying to make that moment disappear
As fear and hatred spread through her body like cancer
She'll never look at men the same way
She wears a bloodstained tattoo that reads…
DAMAGED GOODS

He met the love of his life, so he thought
A home, car, and everything she wanted he bought

Worked like a hey mon…
two, three, and sometimes four jobs at a time
Once she'd received her bachelor's degree,

She announced to him, “I need a man with deep pockets and
swagga.”

He arrived home to discover that all her belongings were gone
His knees hit the hardwood floor as he allowed his heart to
vacate
He’ll never look at women the same way
He wears a bloodstained tattoo that reads…
DAMAGED GOODS
She’s so in love would do anything for him
Aunt Flo, this month was a no show
Positive read on the wand…a oops baby would be born

He said, “I’ll never tell a soul that it is mine.”
Abortion hung on his lips like poisoned wine
As she laid back and placed her feet in the stirrups of death
Tears saturated her hairline as the nurse held her hand

In that moment she received her bloodstained tat that reads…
DAMAGED GOODS
She’ll never look at men the same way

He got her pregnant; decided to step up to the plate

Placed a ring on it and set a date

She made his life miserable

Maybe unintentional distorted his character,

Filled his soul with hate

Psychologically destroyed he swore he'd never marry again

He wears a bloodstained tat that reads…

DAMAGED GOODS

He did a complete 180 when she said, "I Do!"

From her bloody mouth, she shouts for someone, anyone...

PLEASE CALL 911

Her baby cries filled the air as she begged him to stop

The blows increased and still no cops

As blood dripped onto her tattered blouse...

She swore she hated men and would never ever marry again

She wears an izezumi tattoo* that reads…

DAMAGED GOODS

*izezumi tattoo = to insert ink. Japanese tattooing tradition of inserting ink beneath the skin to form the tattoo, said to be painful. Also worn by Yakuza (Japanese gangsters).

DON'T LIGHT THE WICK

This candle's been lit and blown out for the last time
Don't light it if you're not ready for eternity
Don't light it if you can't feed my soul, my mind

Can't handle the extremity of my energy
Don't light the wick

Don't light the wick
If you can't interact in my world,
For I'm not down with temporary flicks

So, don't even think about **lighting this wick**...
If you can't commit

GRANDDADDY CLEO

(For my granddaddy, the Late Cleofus Wheeler R.I.P)

My grandfather was taken home
Many, many years ago
By this disease named cancer
My **Granddaddy Cleo**

So, I wrote a letter
A week after he'd gone
In hopes that he'd hear
The words inked from the pen
Clinched between my fist

I must say,
I'll never go another day
Without verbalizing and shouting
I love you to those in my life
In fear...One of our souls
Will soon take flight

Memories of you hold strong...
In my cranium
Visualizing you standing tall

And smells of your cigar
Vroom-Vroom
Me on my tiptoes peeping
From the window
From the bedroom
Sounds of the cars
You fixed in your backyard

Love for cars manifest from you
Pedal to the metal
I love that too
I was told to call
To say I love you

Didn't understand death
'Til you left

My reflection of you was...
Army strong
Invincible
Unbeatable
Yet there I was
Staring at your coffin
In disbelief

I never got a chance to say, “I love you.”
I wrote it then and saying again
In hope that you’d hear
The words I should have said
Many, many years ago
“I love you, **Granddaddy Cleo**.”

WHAT IF

(For those dreamers such as myself)

What if...

You go for yo' hearts desires

Can't stand the fire

What if...

The storms knock you off track?

You can't find yo' ass back--

Back home to your comfort zone

You're all alone--alone--alone

What if...

The ground crumbles at yo' feet?

You can't find the rhythm; can't find the beat

You get lost--lost in those unfamiliar streets

What if...

You open yo' mouth an

Nothin' comes out

Everyone's staring at you

Looking like booboo

What if...

They talk about you?
Disown you?

What if...

They hate you?
They're all gonna laugh at you--
Laugh at you--laugh at you

What if...

They use your name in vain?
Oh shame, shame, shame
Ahh hell, what if you jus' plain as fail

What if...

The universe, the Divine Power
Yo' God ignore yo' cries--
Of why, why, why?

What if...

You step on that stage
Forget the words to say?

What if...

You forget to breathe?

Come crashin' to yo' knees

Realizin'

This shit ain't comin with ease

WHAT IF, WHAT IF, WHAT IF

What if...

You up root those negative seeds?

Cultivating your - insane in the membrane - your brain

Driving you crazy and derange

What if you…

What if you…

What if you…

What if you

What…if…you, Succeed?

BROKEN RECORD

A record can only repeat the words
So many times, before it's broken

It becomes worn from repeated misuse
Wishin' you would finally
Understand the meanin'
Of the words,
That you could finally
Appreciate its melody
Before...It's broken

The vinyl can only attain its crisp sound
When handled delicately
And repeated misuse is not it…
The song can only play so often
'Til it realizes – that hell you not even listenin'

That song will soon change
Change to a tone,
A beat, sounding much like footsteps walkin' away

A slow fade away
And that fade away in its silence
Will sound like a sonic boom

BEHIND THOSE DOORS

The Devil disguised as a friend
Eased His way into my world
Blindfolded to His motives
To destroy my soul

Brought devastation into my life
Never thought this would happen to me
Things that you see on TV

Who wrote me into this script?
Perpetration
Calculations
Of every move
Clueless to what was waiting
Behind those doors
Tainted my life
My vision of others, friendships, and men
My naivety set my fate

My trustworthiness…
My views…

Forced upon those sheets

I lost my vision

Visions of my life became distorted

My life collapsed

Forced by evil

Into darkness

BEHIND THOSE DOORS

BREAK ME DOWN

Beaten down to a pulp
But **BREAK ME DOWN...**
It will not do

Suffocated my spirit
Diluted my expectations
But **BREAK ME DOWN...**
It will not do

Opened my eyes to the dark side
At every other corner
Introduced me to evils on earth
Locked and bind my heart
My safeguard
But **BREAK ME DOWN...**
It will not do

Almost had me
Closed minded
Cynical

But a Higher Power moved in
Quilted me with His love
A Higher Power's got this

Guided my pathways to
Mental and Spiritual growth

Life's whirlwinds
Every unclear path
Prepared me
Strengthened me
Made me
Optimistic
Spiritual
Stronger
Wiser

His love
Made me
The entity I am today
BREAK ME DOWN...
It'll never do

For He's quilted me
With His love
So, **BREAK ME DOWN...**
It will not do

UNTITLED

God bless the day you came into my life
You stole my heart like a thief in the night

Through the storms, you've been my sun
Your smile…my rainbow
Your body
Your soul
My vessel of gold

You brought stability
And unconditional love into my life
I never had to think twice

I want you to be the first I see when I rise
The last when I close these eyes

I want to be the shoulder you cry on
I am that person you can rely on

Without limitation
I give you all of me
I only ask for a little reciprocity

CHALLENGER

My love for you is
Challenger Deep,
Beyond 35,840 feet…
Below sea level

I'll love you for infinity
Beyond the end of time
This love flows constantly
Through these veins of mine

We're so in sync that your
Private thoughts converse with me,
Your face reveals the tears
That you attempt to conceal

And because my love for you
Is like titanium
I automatically enfold you
When you are weak - I'll be both your feet
Until you can stand tall on your own

I'll be your motion - your wings when yours are broken
Because my love for you is
For eternity,
Infinity
It is never-ending
Everlasting

It is beyond 35,840 feet...
It is
Challenger Deep

WHAT MORE

What more do you want from me
That you haven't already taken?
What more do you want from me
That I haven't already given?

Every inch of my black skin
Every drop of blood
Passed from my kin

Every strand of my black hair
My voice
My intellect
My womb
My sanity
My lost history

What more do you want from me
That you haven't already taken?
How much more do you want from me
That I haven't already unenthusiastically given?

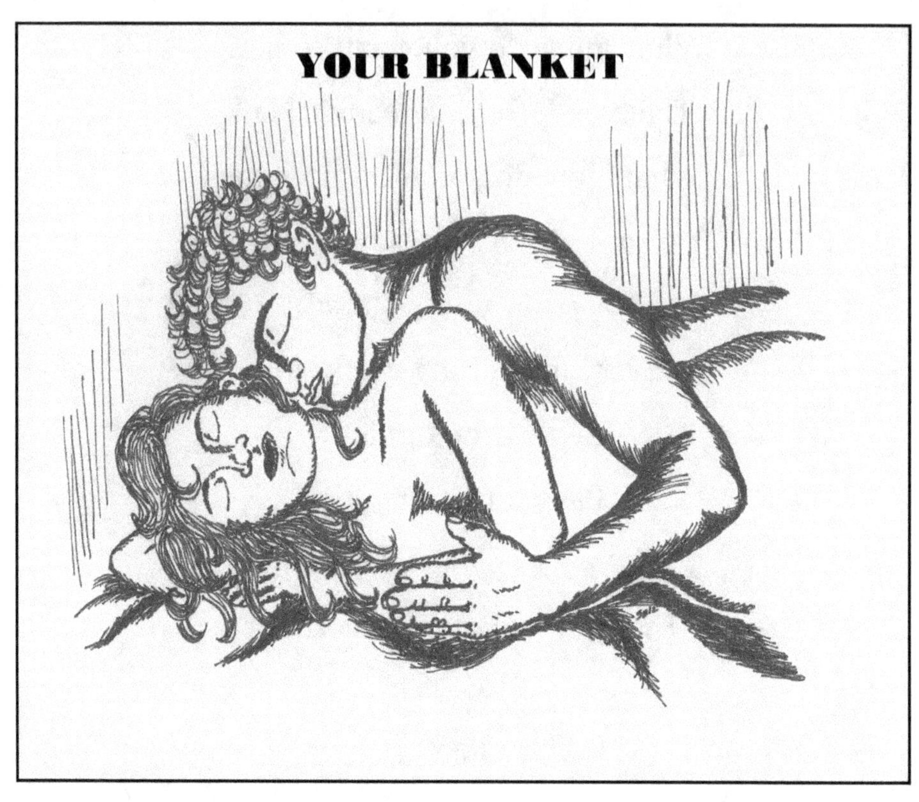

IF I WERE YOUR BLANKET, I'D COVER YOU WITH LOVE
FROM THE TOP OF YOUR HEAD TO THE SOLES OF YOUR FEET.
IF I WERE YOUR BLANKET YOUR DREAMS, I'D KEEP
SAFELY TUCKED WITHIN MY NEVER TO UNRAVEL SEAMS.

YOUR BLANKET

If I were **your blanket**, I'd cover you with love
From the top of your head to the soles of your feet
If I were **your blanket**, your dreams I'd keep
Safely tucked within my never to unravel seams

If I were **your blanket**, I'd gently hold you
As I absorb your falling tears
If I were **your blanket**, I'd caress
And kiss every inch of you

Including the small of your back,
Not excluding the tips of your toes
And those places that special garments...
Have the pleasure to hold

And when I become old and worn
And not as beautiful as the rest
I'd anxiously wait upon the shelf
Praying that you'd choose me
Over the rest

DISTANT MEMORY

As the calls decreased
The I love you's went wit 'em
The heart followed sometime behind
Whole freakin' relationship dramatically ceased

Suffered from congestive heart failure
Not really - severe broken heart - it just felt like it died
And I fought to keep this overly sensitive sucker alive

Tried to catch up...
Get on the same page as you
But I fell further and further behind
I lost count of how many days and nights
Tears and smiles set upon this face
Enough to cause 'em to intertwine
Becoming indistinguishable - -identical
But as the time and the days leave us behind

It becomes harder and harder to find
The reasons I felt I couldn't live without you,
The reasons I cried over you,
The reasons I allowed you to make a fool out of me,
And I am so glad you're now a **distant memory**

EXPLOSIVE

I feel **explosive** energy,
When you're in close proximity

We emerge like waves in the ocean,
And I get wet with every motion

When you're around, I want us to lose control,
And let the passion unfold

I feel the heat with every touch
I want to dance with you by candle light...
If that's not too much

I want us to ignite in the bedroom,
And come together like bodies of water...
Real soon

MOONLIT CRIES

My womb bore unconditional love
Beautiful gift...
From our Creator

The first kick - kick - kick
Covered me with excitement...
Events flashing like snippet flicks

Emotional pain to the highest degree,
My angel was snatched...
Away from me

Countless nights
These moonlit walls
Eavesdropped on my cries
Was so unsure of how to provide for you and I

Yet, I'd been making plans for two
But he had other ideas...
For me and you

Snippets of events flash before my eyes
As I try to conceal...
My **moonlit cries**

WHAT WOULD YOU SAY?

A life will be taken away
Wanted you to stay

Echoes in my head
He'd repeatedly said
He'd have nothing to do with you
What am I to do?

Hate, will you feel for me
For bringing you into this world
Wondered what you'd be
Baby boy or lil' baby girl

He'd be MIA in your life
My decision has to be right
Because it's about your tiny life

So, what am I to do?
When he wants nothing to do with you
How would you feel?
What would you say?
How would you live?
Knowing he didn't want to stay
Knowing that he walked away

DEPRESSION

Suffocating
Walls closing in fast
Decayed memories
Of the past

Defeat after defeat
Draw the blinds
Cover my face with these sheets

Seems, I'm takin' my last breath
Suffocating
Decaying
Can't shake it...
Do they have a pill for this shit?

Every step appears to shift
In the wrong direction
Silent pain
Hidden from those around me
Where does reality lie?
Brokenhearted

Can anyone feel this pain?
Am I in this alone?

I can't breath
Suffocating
Empty
Confused
Depressed
Stressed
Scorn
Broken
Spine crushing
Mind cloggin'

A high spirits leech
Draw the blinds
And cover my face
With the sheets
And just let me sleep

PATHETIC APOLOGIES

Don't darken my doorstep
Your **pathetic apologies**
Are not welcomed here

You abandoned your responsibilities
Few tears were shed here

You carried the scent of a coward
Your disappearance was predictable

You darken my doorstep...
Asking me, wanting me
To open my heart to you

I'll forgive, but never forget
The pain you introduced into my life

Naïve, I allowed it
But it's a new day

Did thoughts sprint and hurdle...

Through that nibble of a brain?
Thoughts that I'd let you back,
Back into my life, yeah right?
Burnt bridges you can't cross twice

You darken my doorstep
To attempt to articulate those
Pathetic apologizes

Hmmph,
You're a little too late

TIME

If we could rewind and freeze **time**
I would rewind it freeze it
Make it hold still

My heart could be my offering,
A window soul for your appraisal

The hours would rewind,
Time would freeze hold still
So, I could evaluate and assess
The true meaning of your heart
So, we could review the
Possibilities of this opportunity

If only we could rewind and freeze **time**
Instead, hours, days, and weeks move forward
And we continue to silently walk-by
Allowing this opportunity and the possibilities
To pass us by

QUICKLY

Life's too short to put on hold
Holding on to something that doesn't...
Want to be held

Move forward toward your dreams
Toward your goals,
Embrace those you love

Time will move rapidly,
Live each day as your last
Move forward from your past

Look back from time to time
Only to see how far you've come
And how you've grown

Get your QT with those you love,
Say all the things you have to say

Time will say goodbye QUICKLY
And you can never get it back

Hold no regrets
Fly free and fly high
Enjoy your view
Because time will
QUICKLY...
Say goodbye

EMINENT LOVE

You possess a **love so eminent** that...
It's impossible for one to imitate

Energy so electrifying it resurrects the soul
And just in case - you've never noticed nor been told

Passion oozes from your pores causing
Attraction from those within your path

Erotic tones stimulate the psyche
As you verbalize your inner thoughts
And F.Y.I. that is the foundation of vibrations...
Between my thighs
Having me secretly screaming OOOOH MYs

Powerful I must say the least -
And I don't think you truly realize the power that you possess
Because I sometimes detect masquerade smiles and laughter

Perhaps, medication or some type of meditation to get
You through those deeply seeded mental upsets
Removal of the space between you and I is mandatory

So, I implement a plan to get to the inner you
Bringing silence to the voices in my head
To discover your inner cries –
So, I can formulate how we can unify

The depths of your eyes narrate a hint of untold stories
Insecurities delicately hidden behind those gorgeous ass eyes

Your heart is on dial requesting that special type of love
Not that disturbed, psycho, stalk yo' ass in the dark...
Kind of love

But that lil' bit of jealousy, every song reminds me of you
And I wake up and go to sleep with you on my mind...
All the damn time...Kind of love

And because you and I are owners of that kind of **eminent love**
That love I SOOO…Need to give you…Yea, that kind of love

You so deserve this kind of love
So, I blow a mist of my love your way
As I await your okay…to send the thunder

SOUL CONNECTION

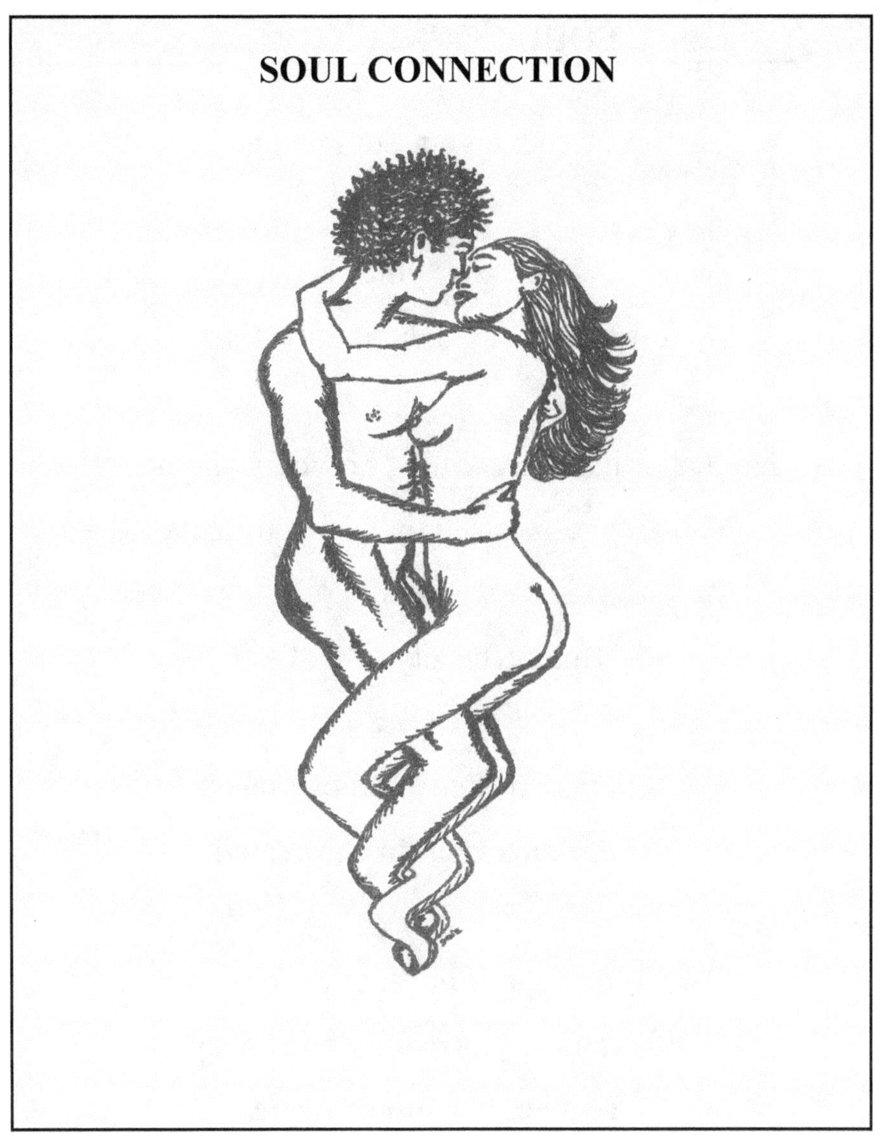

YOU FOUND YOUR COMPLETION

THE ONE

THAT STOPS YOUR FEET

FROM MOVING IN EITHER DIRECTION

SOUL CONNECTION

You found your completion
The One
That stops your feet
From moving in either direction

No matter how fast or how far you want to run
You are mesmerized by its magnificence

But the beauty of it all,
The One
Is just as captivated by you
Your souls remain connected

Thousands of miles away
Effortlessly **your souls** find a way
To silently **communicate**

No need for words…
Your desires manifest
As **your souls** reveal
Each other's request

Creating some form of
Chi energy
A type of Kinetic energy

Whichever, it may be
Electric energy
As molecules vigorously
Shift between the two of you

INVASION

My darkness was **invaded** by light…
Sunlight…
Content in my darkness,
So, I thought

Under attack in a unique form
A beam that shined on areas
Bringing understanding
And growth to self

Sunshine is its name
It runs parallel to me soul
Beautiful is its name
In all its uniqueness
Love is what I call it
Equivalent to me,
Yet different in its own

It's the sun in my darkness
The breath inhaled into my
Corpselike soul

It's the invasion that brought
Light into the dark areas of my life

THE ESSENCE OF…

I want to capture every **essence of your mind, body, and soul**
I want to be that fire that burns in your heart
That energy that enlightens your soul

I want to be the softness from your lips to mine
That passion in every touch, each wave of every motion

I want to capture every **essence if your mind, body, and soul**
I want to be the tenderness in your voice
That warmth in your smile

I want to be the whirlwinds of every emotion
That excitement in your eyes, the wetness in every tear

I want to be the sweet taste of your body
That knowledge held in your dome

I want to consume every **essence of your mind, body, and soul**
Until we are whole

TOXIC

Our past followed us into this union
The disappointments, pains from our prior loves
The ones we thought completed us
The ones we thought made us whole
The loves we said we'd grow old together
And die together

Our past followed us into this union
The union of you and I
And it became you, I...
And an invisible them

Our love will rise above it all
All the heartaches and mistakes
All the tears
Empty words
Words thrown at each other like stones
Our love will withstands it all

$1,200 subtracted by $1,500 equals a negative 300
Subtract 300 more for that broken glass in the back door

$600 we owe
Through the repos and bill collector calls
Our love will rise above it all

The gossip on the street...
Is that someone's been
Cheating between the sheets
Someone's been working overtime
Yet, the mortgage is behind

Special ring tones and one ring hang-ups
What's that all about?
Our past followed us into this union
The deceits, the lies, distrust
I think I smell his or her musk

Prior **toxic** associations
Spilled over into our love
Our past is trying to destroy this union
But believe that our love will rise above it all
I guess?

WITHOUT PERMISSION

Unwilling to immerse you into my soul
They unified **without my permission**
Emerging like waves dancing to shore
They're in sync
Without my permission

Enjoying every wet moment
Every touch, passionately placed
Sending small intense electric pulses
Through my anatomy
Up and down my spine
Physically we have never touch
Not even, close
Nevertheless, our souls found a way
To encounter each other
Without my permission

I refuse to inject you
Yet, I feel your spirit
Flowing through my veins
Pulsating in and out of my heart
Without my permission

You live within me
Without my permission

Without my permission
My heart fell in love with you

Without my permission
My soul unified with you…
Without my permission

SMOOTHNESS

There's ***smoothness*** in everything you do
So damn **smooth** you're considered a taboo

Add your gift of gab to ya swagga' baby
Multiply it to your style of dress
Plus, your super sexy smile
And Oh yes, those Lips - Lips - Lips
Equals a colossal amount of irrefutable style

Rhythmic is how every word
Flows off your tongue
Reason number one for why I'm
Hanging on every word you deliver

If I could capture your voice on tape
I'd use it to meditate

It is truly amazing how your physique
Complements your intelligence, so perfectly

Yes, Yes, Yes

Smoothness is in everything about you
The reason men sit around cogitating on how you...
Seamlessly do the things that you do

While the women are vividly marinating
On how deep your ***smoothness*** can go

MEMORANDA

People misuse, abuse, and throw the word love around
Because they don't understand it

Love is more than a feeling
Feelings come and go like gas bubbles

It's living and being for each other
It's inhaling that individual into your soul...
AND NEVER EXHALING!

FABRICATION

A **fabricated** dream within the walls of my brain
A dream I've suddenly woke up from
Attempting to return to a comatose state
To recapture my fantasy

Yet, it seems it's long gone
A creation of my imagination -
Your perfection

An illusion?
Were you flawlessly molded?
Perfectly **fabricated** within the walls of my mind -
Conclusion?

NONE OF THE ABOVE

She said, “Excuse you” as she rolled her head.
Do I have fool stamped in the middle of my forehead?
Do you honestly think I believe every line I’m fed?

Does it look like I can’t distinguish night from day?
Do you think I survive off of hay?
‘Cuz you sure keep throwin’ it my way,
Like I was born yesterday

Have you ever seen me suckin’ my thumb
Or do you think I’m just plain dumb?

Whatever the case may be
Open your eyes to see
I am none of the above
You can’t show me love
Get on like you been spit on

Don’t worry I won’t shed a tear
Cause frankly, my dear
I’ve gotten sick of you being
Up and in
And all around
My ear

TICK TOCK

TICK…TICK…TICK…TOCK
The time on the clock

Passes like molasses
Astronomically slow
As slow as it can go

Almost to a complete stop
That clock in the hall on the wall
TICK…TICK…TICK…TOCK

Too many **ticks** in-between those **tocks**
Every clock under the cosmos
Goes like molasses as time passes
Just watchin', watchin', watchin'
Waitin' and countin' waitin' and countin'

Every second of every minute
Of every hour on the hour
To breathe again
TICK…TICK…TICK…TOCK

BEYOND THE SKY

Looking **beyond the sky,** I often think of you
Your lovely smile and warm embrace
I retain so many memories of you

I loved you with all my heart
But certain circumstances kept us apart

You had to go your way
I had to go mine
Paths cross from time to time

In a dream, in reality, at the corner of some unknown street
Ten or twenty years from now, again we shall meet

Your dreams I hope come true
I hope you realized I loved you

I'M OF THE NIGHT
HOURGLASS SHAPED
CHARMING AND GENTLE
BUT IF YOU DARE DISTURB MY WEB
OR DARE TO MISUSE ME
I'LL EXPOSE YOU TO MY MACABRE ACTIVITIES

BLACK WIDOW

I'm of the night
Hourglass shaped
Charming and gentle
But if you dare disturb my web
Or dare to misuse me
I'll expose you to my macabre activities

Entangle you into my web
Perform my mating ritual
Triple inject your ass
With my poisonous venom

Seductive kisses to the back of your neck
Landing you flat on your back
Paralyzing you with my poisonous bites
Yes, with those kiss you like

And I'll seductively kiss you
Again, and again
Then nest above you
As my venom
Brings you
To your dying end

YOU ARE

You are my shelter in a time of storm
You gave me a shoulder to cry on

You are my cool breeze on a hot summer day
You are my burning fire on a cold winter night

You are my backbone when I can't hold my head high
You are my beautiful butterfly

You cut my puppet strings
You healed my broken wings

You are the missing puzzle piece...
That completes my life
You are my food...
When I need to be fed

You are my growth
You are my confidant
You are my best friend…my homie
You are

WORKPLACE CULTURE CONFLUENCE

A building...An office space
Our workplace
Combined of different worlds

Red, yellow, brown, white, black
His hip-hop gear
To his polo slacks
His Mi Amor to her my love

Her submissiveness to her self-assertiveness
Her covered from head to toe
To her I'm free to be me
To wear my skirt anywhere above my knees

Behaviors, beliefs, roles, rules, ethics, age groups
Young culture, old culture
Combined together to accomplish one goal

To satisfy customers of different worlds
To produce revenue
For one company
In a building...In an office space
We call our workplace

LOVE JUST DOES

Love just does

When it is needed, it doesn't wait to be asked

Love just does

Love is more than a feeling; it is an action, it is passion

It is beauty, it is doing, it is...

Love thinks of its' love's needs before it thinks of another's

Love just does without being asked or told

Because love knows...love just knows...

DECEIT

He fell in love with this girl
Center of his world

She studied the world's geography
By going state to state on shopping sprees
He suffered financially
Only to see her smile

He received a picture text
Of his wife having sex

He looked closely at the pic
To discover that his wife
Had been with his best friend

"I treated him jus' like a brother."
He said, "How could you do me this way?
Deceive me in such a way?"

They held their heads low
With nothing to say

She trusted her best friend
Like no other
They shared their secrets and dreams
Among one another
Their bond was strong
'Til she found out she'd been
Bon—in' her lover

She asked 'em,
"How long has this been goin' on?"
Their reply, "A week after we met."

She ask her,
"How could you do me this way?
Deceive me in such a way?"

They held their heads low
With nothing to say

CELEBRITY

(For those that shine in the spotlight)

I am a **celebrity**
Not only
For money
Not only
For the fame
Although you may
Feel that was my only
Aim

I chose it
And it chose me
To bring healing
To self and others
It chose me
As I chose it

To bring beauty
To bring laughter and
Momentary happiness

To bring awareness
To the things some
Are never exposed to

You labeled me a **celebrity**
Mentally removing
Me from humanity

I am not a gargoyle
I am still human
With
Human pains
Human disappointments
Human sorrows
Human loneliness

My cheeks get wet too
My trials and tribulation
Sometimes triple
In accumulation
You seem to forget
I am still apart of humanity
Although you've labeled me
A **celebrity**

TOO FAST

She had to grow up too fast

Taking on a motherly occupation

Although she'd never given birth

Had to hurry home from school

To complete her duties

Puttin' warm food on the kitchen table

She had to grow you too fast

She tried to rebel

Tried to find her voice

But it got lost

In the death

Death of her childhood

Death of her mother

She had to grow up too fast

She felt the world

Wanted her to fail

Couldn't found the glory

In the strength she'd gained

Could not see the beauty in her struggle

Having to care for her father and brother

She'd been thrown into adulthood
Forced to grow up too soon
She went to visit her mother's grave
Only to discover a headstone
Where her childhood's life laid

ADULT HIGH SCHOOL

Barging in 10 minutes late
Dreading to walk through the doors
Half of your peers are fake
The other half flakes

Boss riding your back
So close
The two of you
Look attached

He say-she say
In your ear all day

Politics in
Upper management
HR interviews of
Harassments

Passed over
Looked over
Adult High School

Favoritism
Rumor city
Having to ask
To have the knives
Removed from your back

Overseers
Throwing authority around
Pencil whoopin'
Misusing
And
Abusing

All while smiling all up
And around your face
Perhaps it's happening in your workplace

RETIREMENT

(For the baby boomers)

Goin' into early **retirement**
Don't need anymore
PTO Time
Vacation time
Cause I'm gonna take...
Permanent time

Over 25 years every day
Clocking in at the same 'ol place
Imma go into early **retirement**
A penalty I'll happily take
Jus' so I don't have to make
Another trip to this place

Imma use my free time
To write a book or two
Invest in something new

Spend time with my family
Go visit places I've never seen before

Money may be a little tight
No worries, no choice...
I'll be alright
Cause I'm still going through with
My early **retirement**

No need for anymore
PTO time
Vacation time
Cause I'm gonna take...
Permanent time

STEP OUTSIDE OF YOURSELF

Step outside of yourself

Examine yourself

And evaluate your actions

Along with the words that you speak

Review those thoughts

That flow from the stem of your dome

-Step outside of yourself

To understand the reactions

Fueled by your spoken words or your actions

Step outside of yourself

Examine your reaction

To certain expressions

Visiting you from festering affairs

Causing that agonizing agitation in your mental

Step outside of yourself

Shed your skin

And assess yourself

Before you being

To fault someone else

For something

That was deeply

Rooted within

DICTATORS

Don’t allow your destiny to be defined
By **dictators** and nay-sayers
Mapping out your life
As if they were your Creator

Don’t allow nay-sayers to corrupt your mind
Ruining your faith in God’s plans for you
Speaking of things, they do not understand
As if, God called them into His holy throne
To get their okay for your life's plan

Some mean no harm
By transferring their fears onto you
Causing you to procrastinate
Quit on yourself
On your Creator

Keep **dictators** and nay-sayer out of your inner circle
They’ll keep you trapped in fear
A hostage in your own mind
Delaying your moment in time

HARMONY

My I's are no longer me

My I's are we

And I is no longer living in **harmony**

Never want to utter the words of love

Thus far it's been everything but like the Heaven's above

Rain constantly pouring down my face

Tired of this race

This race between me, he, she, and sometimes we

My I's were no longer me

My I's were we

And since my I's are no longer, we

I'm living in **harmony**

DON'T

Don't justify
Don't entertain me
With your excuses
With your reasons
It is...What it is
And we'll let be...What it be

Don't patronize me
Insult me
Feeding me apologies
And rationalities

Don't give me intangible
Memories
Just don't
I repeat

Don't justify
Entertain or offer
Excuses and your reasoning
They do nothing for me
Nor for my hurt feelings

ALL SHE KNEW

He's left her more times than we can count

She said she wanted out

But he's **all she knew**

He's left her more times than we can count

Left her wondering around a dark and cold house

She screamed she wanted out

But he's **all she knew**

Afraid of freedom

Afraid of peace of mind

Afraid of what would happen

If she were to leave

Afraid she wouldn't survive without him

Afraid of loneliness

Not realizing

That she was already

Making it on her own

Failing to realize that...

She's already in her relationship alone

See he's left her more times than we can count
And when he's there
His mind is somewhere else

She says she wants to leave
But she's afraid to move her feet

Afraid of the unknown
And right now, as you read poem
She's once again home alone

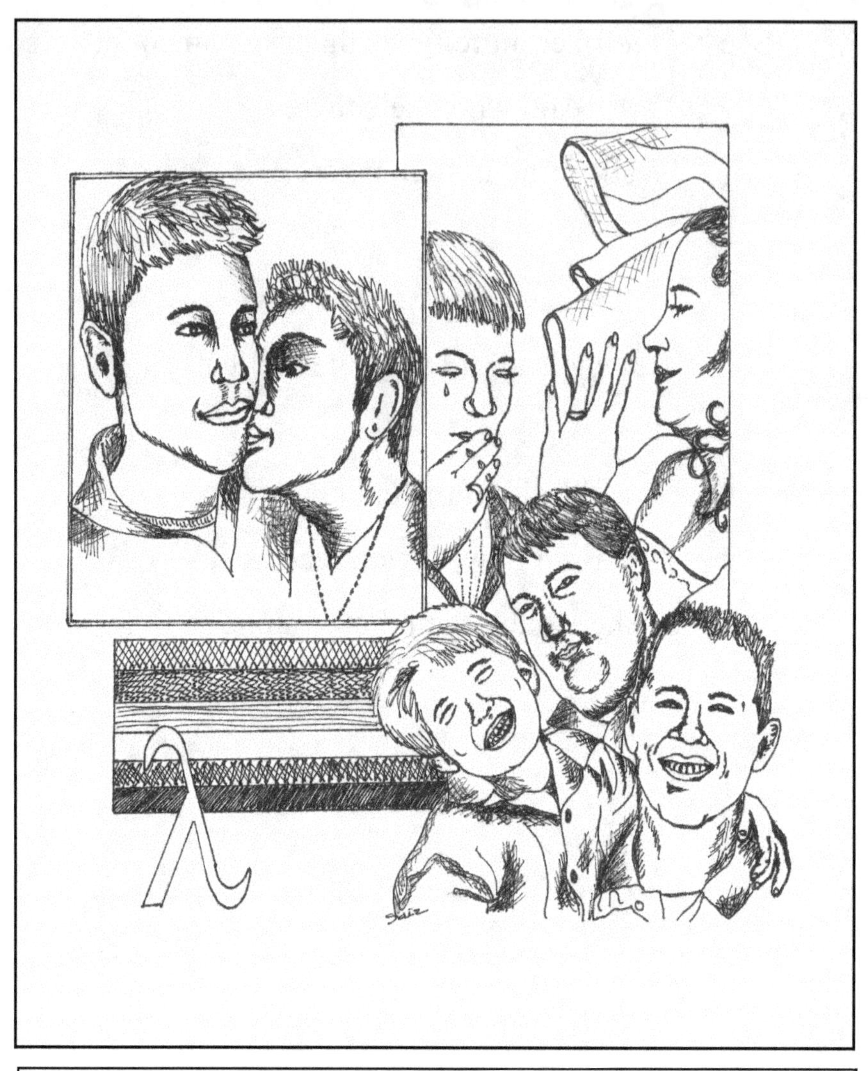

YOU JUDGE ME

BY YOUR IDEAS OF

WHAT'S RIGHT AND WRONG

ATTEMPT TO KEEP ME ISOLATED

BECAUSE I WALK IN MY TRUTH

TO LIVE IN TRUTH

(For D'Law (R.I.P) & the LGBT community)

You judge me
By your ideas of
What's right and wrong

Attempt to keep me isolated
Because I walk **in my truth**

You criticize me
Because my family
Doesn't fit into your idea of
The norm of a nuclear family

You say I made a choice
To have half the world hate me
Refuse to understand me
To have my family possibly disown me

You say I made a choice to have others
Not sit and converse with me
In fear that others will think they're just like me

You say I made a choice to be beaten
Because I love differently.
To fight the world and your laws every day of my life

You say I made a choice to have to fight to
Marry the love of my life

My Creator made me perfectly
Contrary to your belief
I'm different from you
As you are different from me

And I don't have No Damn mental disease!
I'm going **to live in my truth**
With no apologies

And I'm going to shout it loud!
Shout it proud!
I chose **to live in my truth**
And not in you lie

I chose to follow my heart
And love from my heart
Instead of living miserable
In your idea of what's right

Yes, I made a choice **to live in my truth**
Instead of living in your lie

Shadow walkin'
Lightly steppin'
Corner duckin'

SHADOW WALKIN'

Shadow walkin'
Lightly steppin'
Corner duckin'
So, no one can see
Dimmed light
Withdrawn energy

Hoping no one notices
You
Corner duckin'
Shadow walkin'

Hoping no one notices
You trying to walk
Down life's
Roads
Undetected
Invisible to the world
Shadow walkin'
Corner duckin'
So, no one can see

Hoping no one notices

You

Walkin’ down life’s

Roads

Lifeless

In a state of

Invisibility

WE COULD...

(For Sondra Brown-Johnson)

We could stand here and verbalize a thousand consoling words... recite scripture after scripture specifically designed for grievance.

You can gratefully receive a thousand beautifully written sympathy cards.

And we can express how some of us sympathize and others empathize with you in this moment of bereavement. And only someone who's lost that person that was like your left lung could understand that without it it's difficult to breathe. And there are NOT enough consoling words to fill the void that's left in your hearts. And there are NOT enough sympathy cards that could turn back the pages of your lives when it was whole.

Yet we desperately seek for ways to alleviate your heartache.

We desperately seek for ways to bring laughter into your world....to redirect your inner thoughts.

We could stand here and verbalize a thousand consoling words. But we won't...because they're only words.

They cannot rewind the hands of time when your lives were whole.

But we will stand here to remind you that you have family and friends that will walk this journey with you...that you have many silent ears willing to listen to your inner emotions and shoulders to cry on...just pick one or has many as you need...And we'll stand here to let you know that we're present because of the love we have for you and your family.

And Sondra, we'll stand here to let know you can call at 3 o'clock in the morning and we can just breathe into the phone...let we use to do in elementary school.

And that's truth...No lie in it.

DEADLY ABC'S

I am an alphabet killer
A deadly ABC
You know one of those STDs

I can live undetected for years
My mission…destroy T cells on sight

My goal…weaken your immune system
Leaving your body vulnerable
For disease and other ABCs like *PCP, TB, and HPV

I've claimed over a million lives and plan to claim more
Some of you live with me and don't even know
I'm unstoppable baby!

*ARVs can only slow me down
You better keep yourself updated on *cdc.gov
Get yourself tested and use that latex glove
Find out how it's going down in and around your town

Get those stats of where I'm at
Cause ba--by I'm growing into a major epidemic
Don't be naïve and continue to believe that I discriminate
Age, race, gay, or straight, your demise, I cannot wait
You better think wise on that lil' hot date

Without a doubt,
I'm here to wipe the world out

I am universal, baby
I'm one of the deadliest ABC's - a deadly STD

I am that monster
I am that beast
I am that incurable H-I-V

PCP: Pneumonia, TB: Tuberculosis, HPV: Human Papillomavirus
cdc.gov/actagainstaids
ARV: antiretroviral drugs

The Love Column

Lopsided Relationship

Dear L

Mutual love and respect, the existence of those two things always somersaulted in my head. Can two people equally love, care, and respect each other? Or is this only a fairy tale. The key word…EQUALLY! It always seems that someone loves the other more. That someone was putting 120% into a relationship when the other was lagging behind. You'll put an extra 80% to fill the void. Topping you off to 200%, meaning they ain't doing jack shit. There seemed to always be one more considerate, more dependable.

You know what I'm talking about when one is giving all they've got.

Truly,
Mutual Love Seeker

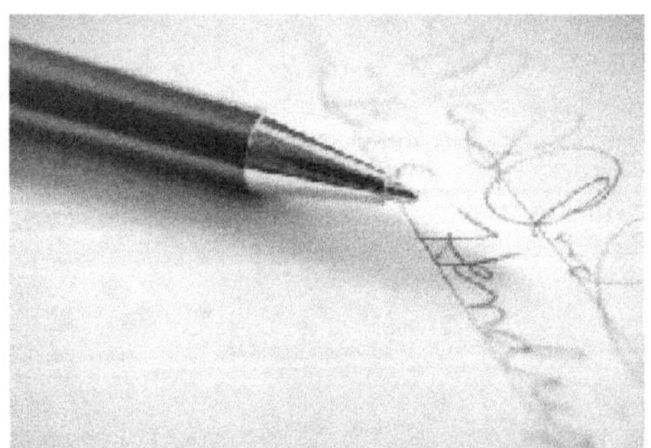

You've fallen victim to a lopsided relationship. Yes, I said a lopsided relationship.

Now some of us have fallen victim to a lopsided relationship more than once and some more than others. Some of us turn into love leeches, just sucking the love out of the other. The victim turned leech is trying to refill from having all the love sucked out of them, from those love predators.

Now here's a short story I like to tell from time to time. There was a girl who will remain nameless who loved with her heart wide open. She was afraid of being alone. Never giving herself time to heal from the leeches destruction. Every relationship she went into carrying those wounds. She never warned others that she was under love construction. She presumed and they assumed she was mentally available. She damaged not only herself but also those in her path. She performed modification after modification until she was lost in herself. She combined her newfound control issues with her insecurities. Smothering others with questions of where you been, why you didn't call, why you didn't answer my call the first time? And it doesn't take you that long to go to the store and back. A panty sniffer is what I call 'em. But in her case ball sniffer…maybe? Needless to say her actions resulting in her running the right ones away. Either you change them or they change you. Most of the time unfortunately the good ones end up damaged. And they end up messing up with that right one or allow the opportunity to pass them by. Get rid of the lopsided relationship one way or another. Mutual love is somewhere out there waiting on you.

The Love Columnist

The Wait

I stand alone on the peak of Mt. Everest
arms wide open to the Heavens.
Respectful screams to my God escape my lips.
"What journey are we embarking now?"
I rewind the adventures of my life,
to take a glimpse of how I've grown into my faith.
No longer questioning why or why me,
for I see how He's carried me.
My conversations with my God are held privately,
just He and me.
He is my Father, my number one dude, my bff,
my number one fan and He is mine.
And I am selfish with our private time.
See, my God, my bestie has carried me
through miles of unwanted sorrows.
He has prepared me for the answer
to the question that follows,
Benign or malignant?
As I await the answer,
I continue to maneuver through life with grace.
I continue to move forward in my space.
No longer moving backwards nor in circular motions

and definitely not in slow motion.
No time for negativity or
unnecessary conversations that serve no purpose.
But to evict the peace residing within my head space.
Wakeup call or not.
I run this race with purpose and grace.
Tryin' to escape with my life like a fugitive.
Because It's time sensitive.
If it takes everything from me
If my health dissipates.
As I await, the answer to the question that follows.
Benign or malignant?
I will still converse privately with my God,
just He and me.
Wakeup call or not.
I'll fight with dignity
to my very last breath.
Even if I have nothing left.
I stand alone on the peak of Mt. Everest
arms wide open to the Heavens.
Respectful screams to my God escape my lips.
"What journey are we embarking now?"
I rewind the adventures of my life,

to take a glimpse of how I've grown into my faith.
No longer questioning why or why me,
for I see how He's carried me;
With the strength of my God, I stand and await,
the answer to the question that follows.
Benign or malignant?

ABOUT THE AUTHOR...

Tonika Yvonne Wheeler known as Toni to family and friends is the founder of BluLibra Entertainment, an independent film company where she writes and produces indie shorts, features, and promotional videos. She's also written for aol.com and she's the brilliant opinion writer of the blog 'Outside the Box' for the online magazine View Woman. In addition, she's performed in numerous plays, indie films, and television. The former behavior adjustment teacher is the mother of one young adult, oldest sister of two siblings, wife, and daughter. Tonika was born and raised in Longview, TX. She's lived in California and currently lives with her husband in the Dallas, TX area.

Note from author:

Overcoming her battle with cancer gave her a new perspective on life and caused her to shift gears. Rather, we know it or not, everyone is battling something. Most of us can relate to being damaged at one point or another in our life. Winning that battle depends on how we approach it. Tonika admits to being Damaged Goods, but not broken.

"Get your power back." ~ Tonika Yvonne Wheeler

SCAN ME